# This Coloring book Belongs to:

_____

# Lamia

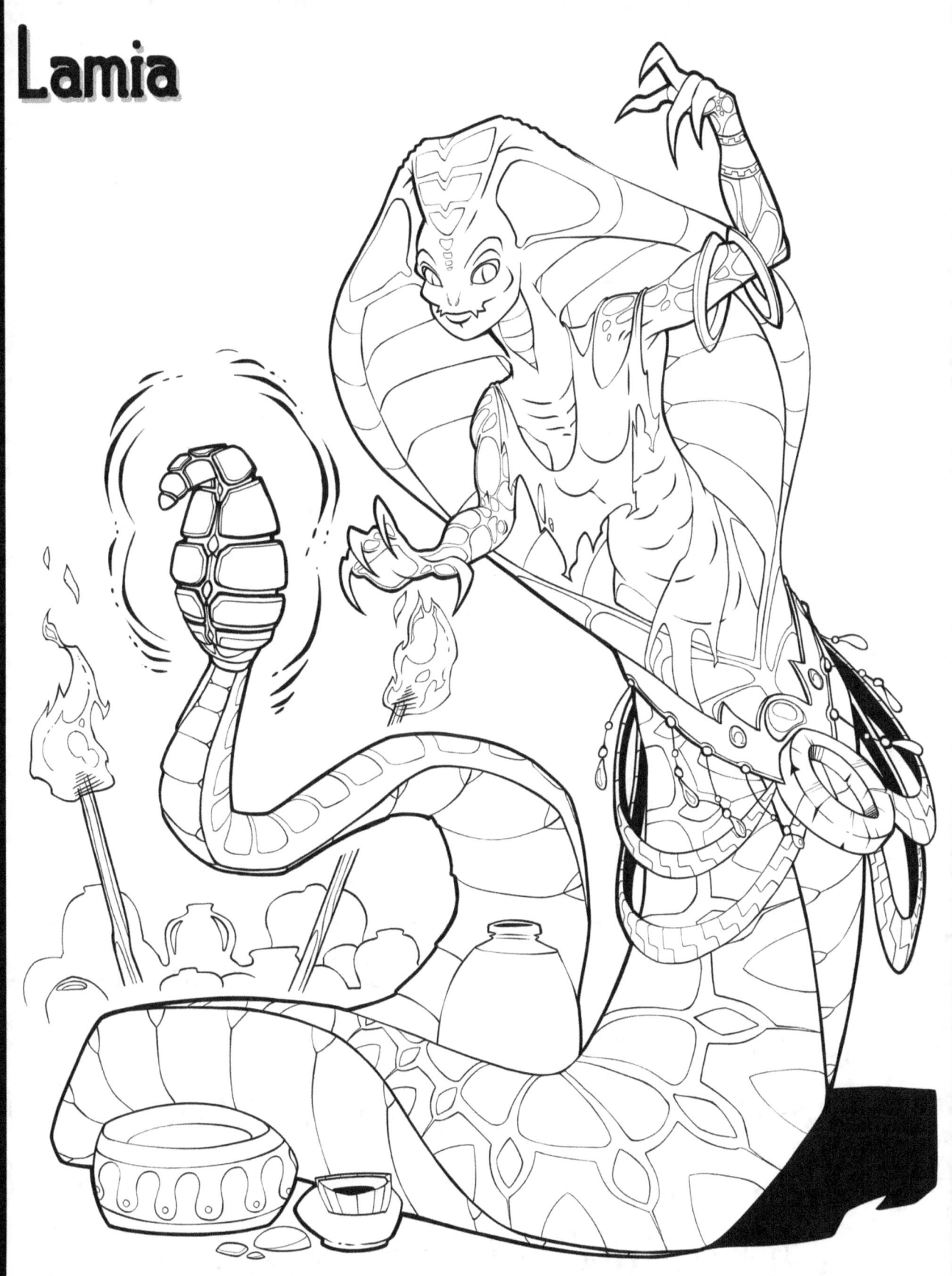

**Lamia:** Parents be weary! This child-eating daemon is out for retribution for the misfortunes she endured at the hands of Hera. With all her offspring being ripped from her, she now yearns to take any child to try and fill her maternal void the maternal void.

# Ettin

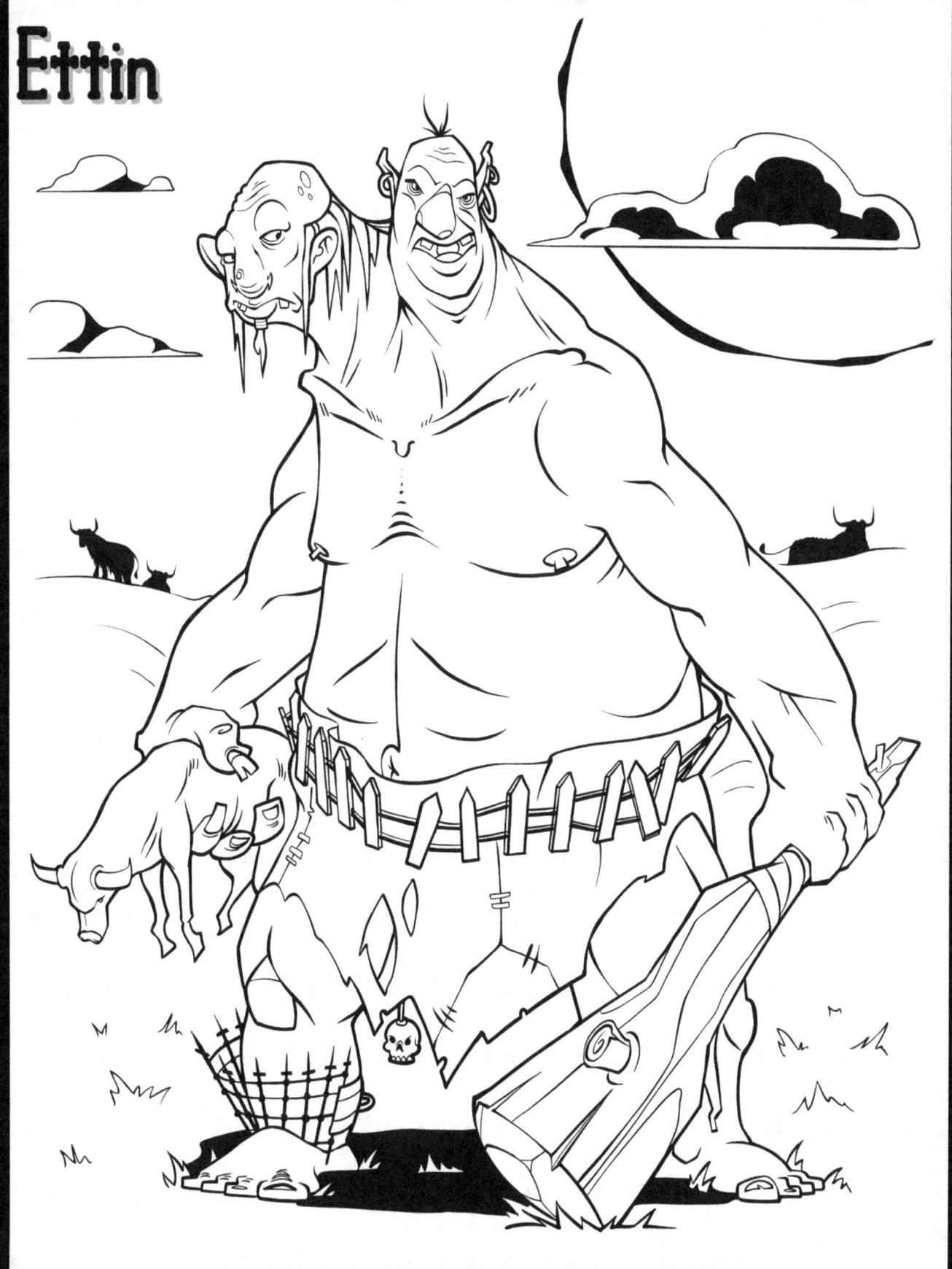

**Ettin:** Commonly known as the two-headed giant, these large creatures are the bullies of the mythical world. Their large and brutish stature helping them push around their victims and destroy their foes. Take peace in knowing that even with two heads, they arn't as quick witted as a giant with one.

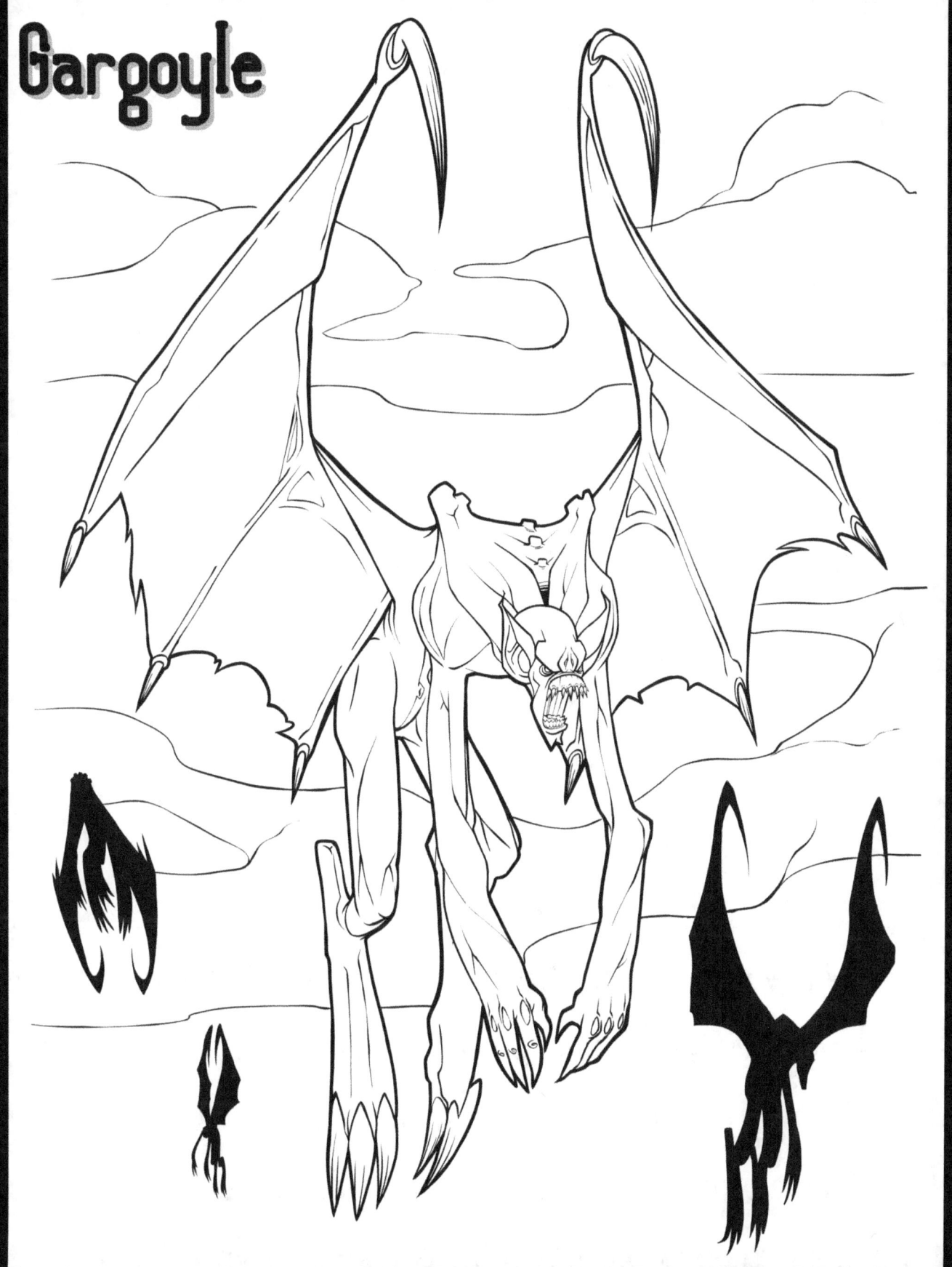

Gargoyle

Gargoyle: These statue-like stone creatures are created with winged backs and devilish looks. They enjoy nothing more than to frighten those around them when they break out of their statuesque poses. Look once, they are statues. Look again, and they're flying at you.

# Cerberus

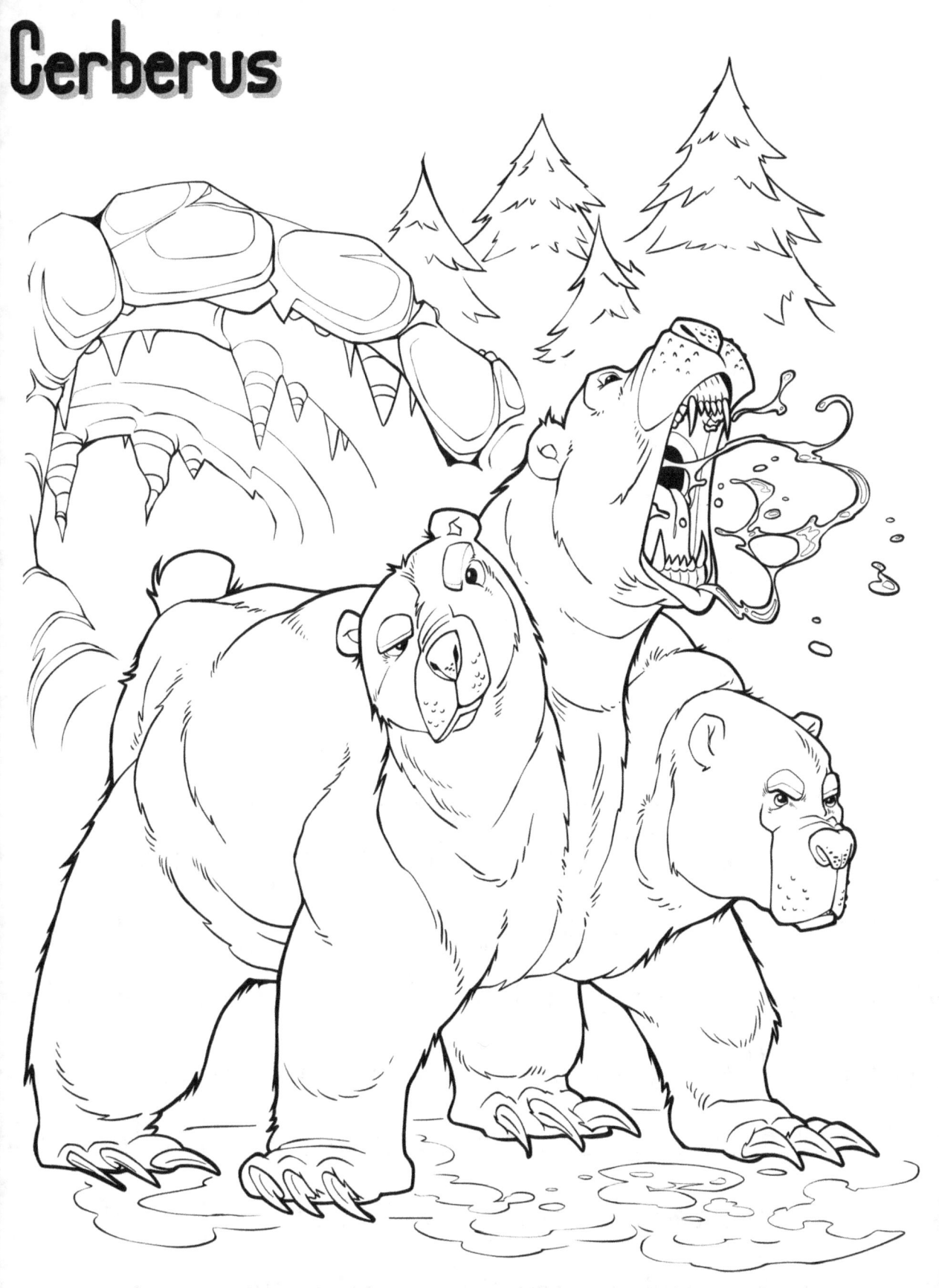

**Cerberus:** The traditional cerberus is the three-headed guard dog of the gates of Hell. These damned hounds will only let the undead pass into the depths of the inferno and those who wish to cross without permission will feel their demonic wrath. This twisted-cerberus took a wrong turn and mutated into the hellfire three-headed bear.

# Gibbering Mouth

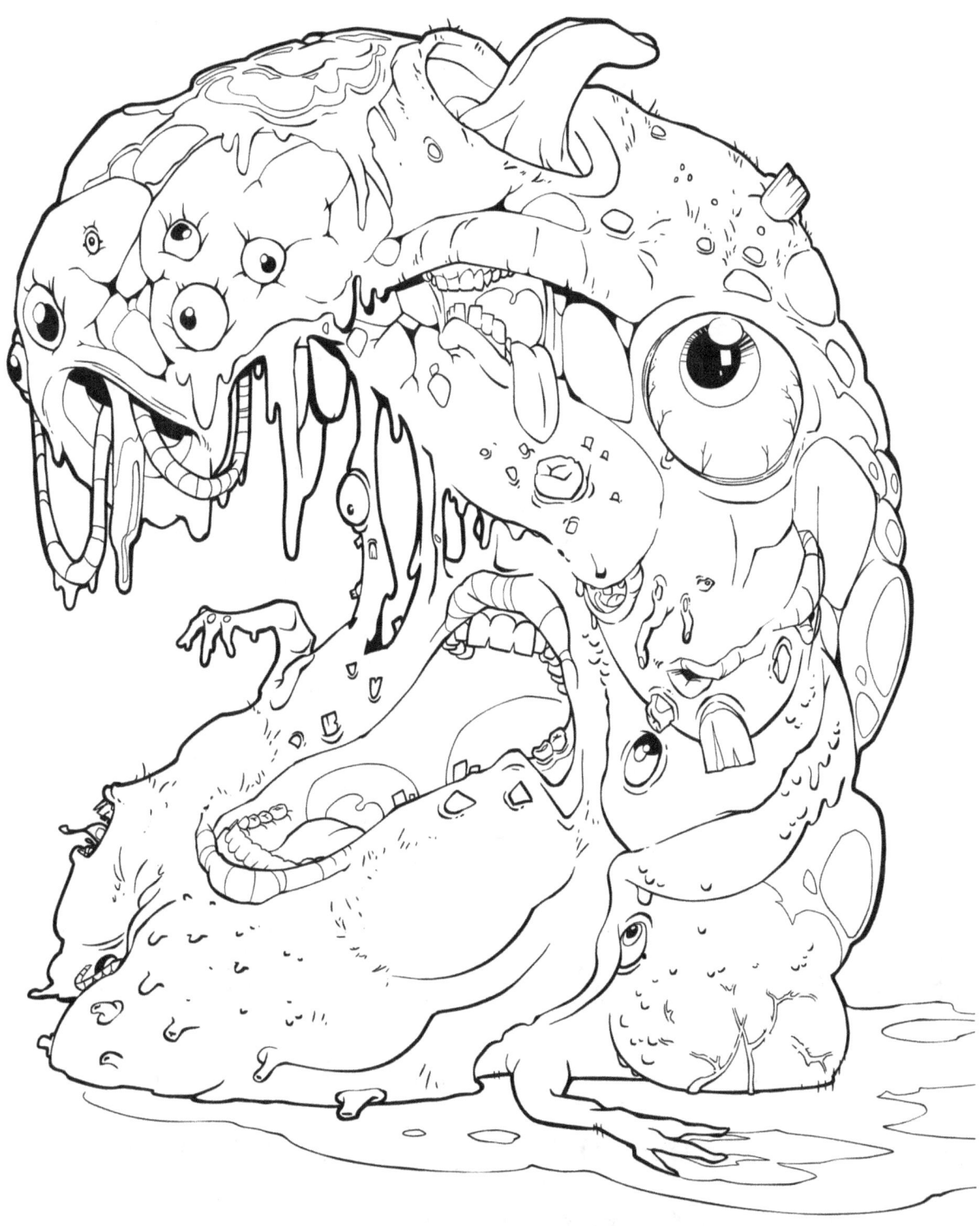

**Gibbering Mouth:** This Monster appears as a large gelatinous blob of gnashing mouths and peering eyes, its only natural drive to consume anything within mouths reach, its appetite utterly insatiable.

# Mimic

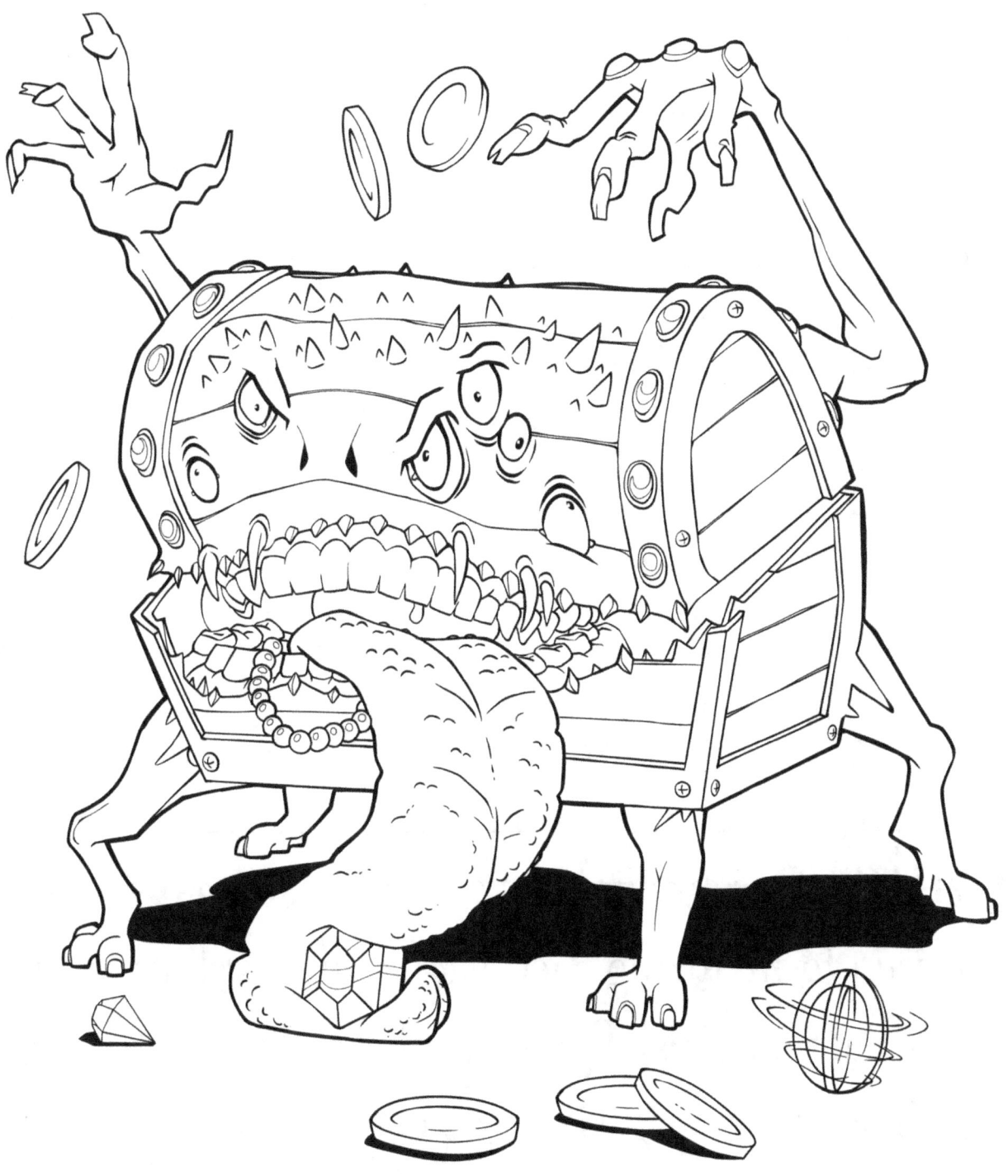

**Mimic:** This amorphous creature can shapeshift into its desired form, luring their victims in by playing on the unfortunate natures of greed and lust. Watch out! Once it adheres to you, it will stop at nothing to make sure their presentation is something you can not deny.

# Manticore

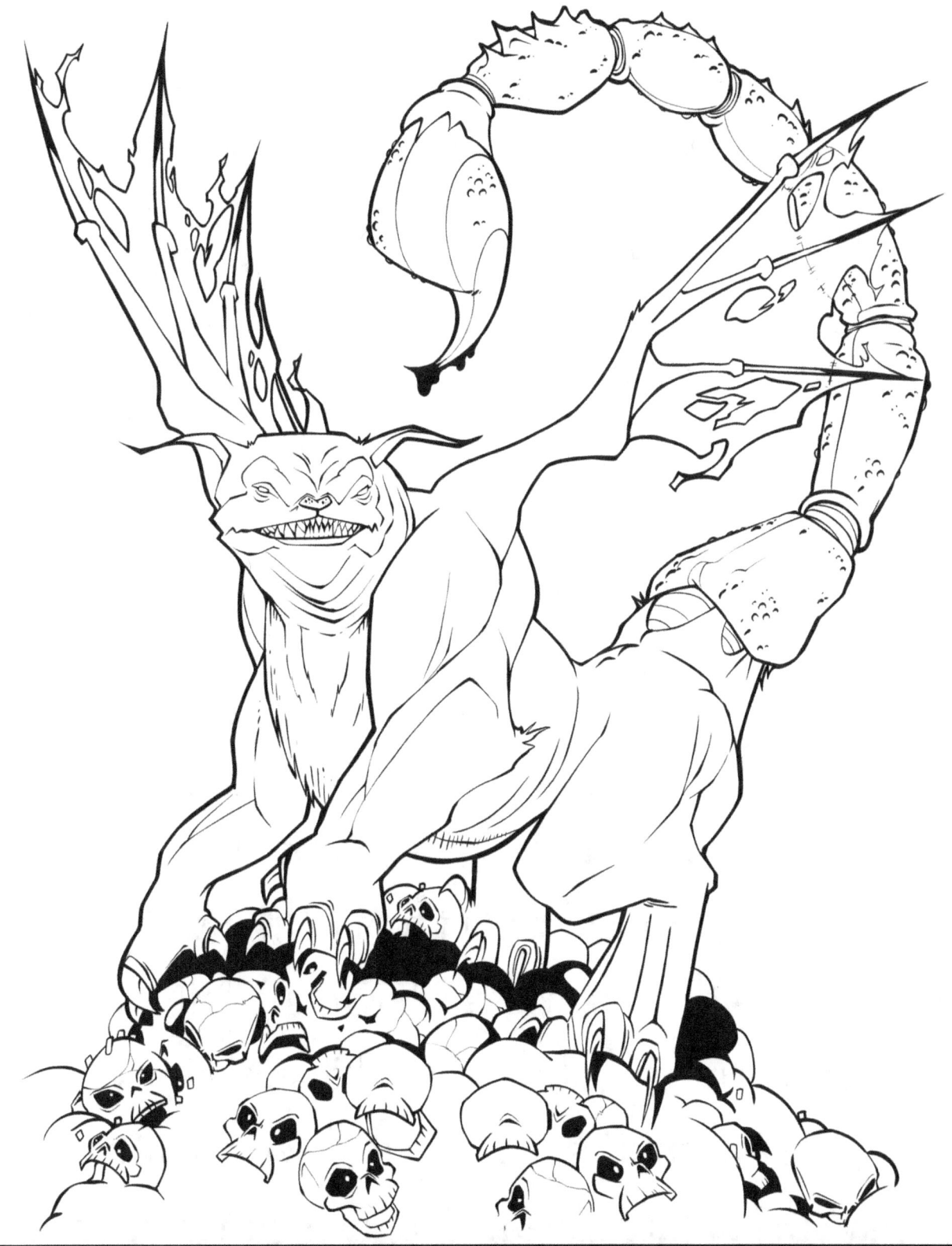

**Manticore:** One of the truest monsters, a manticore has the deformed head of a man, the body of a lion, the wings of a dragon and the terrifying tail of a scorpion. Folklore states that these intelligent beings worked alongside evil entities to bring suffering to those who have the unfortunate luck of being their victim.

# Sand Worm

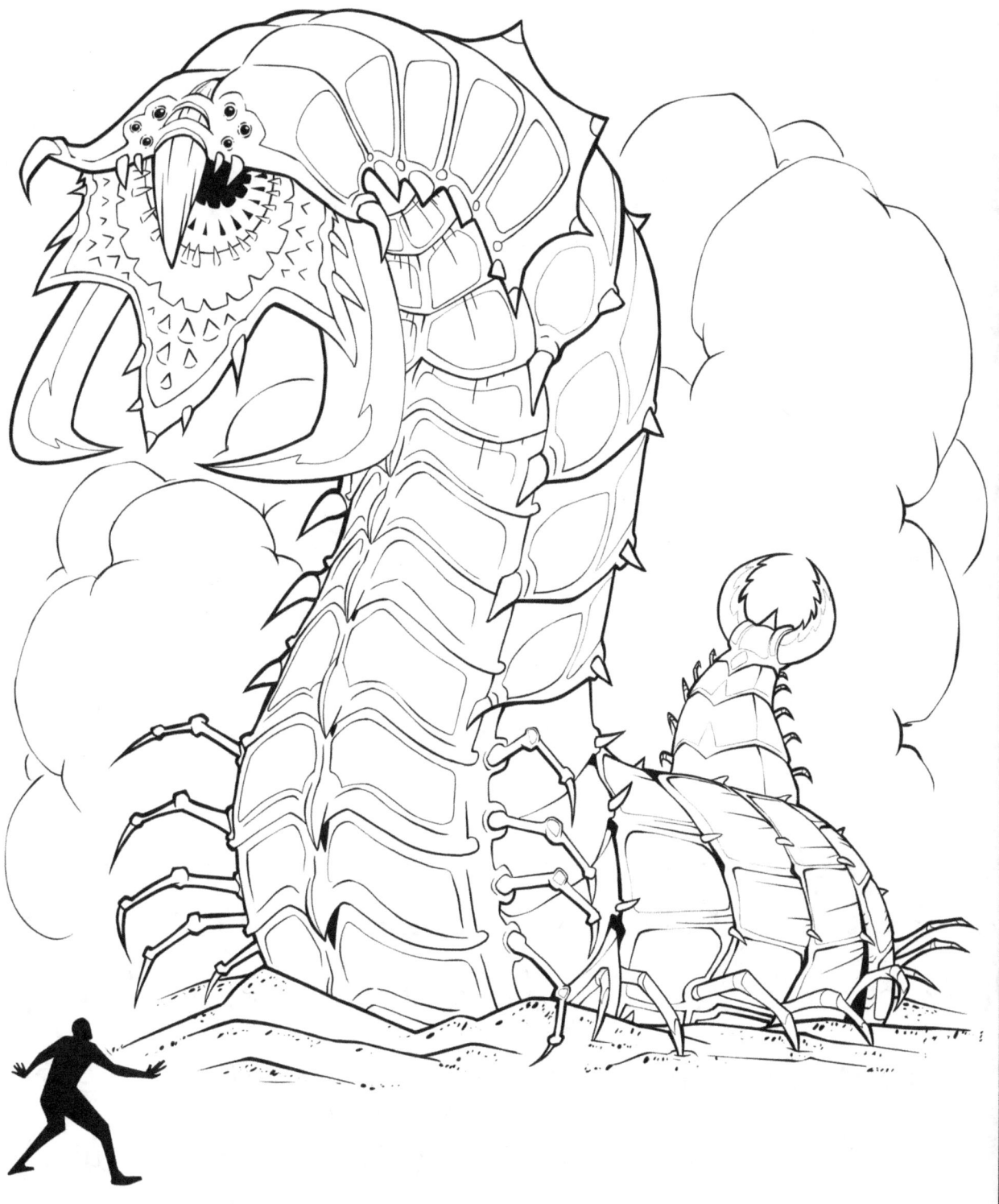

**Sand Worm:** These lethal worm creatures bring destruction to those who decide to cross on to their desert territory. Their ability to travel above and below ground can make for some interesting encounters. If the sand below your feet starts to tremble, beware!

# Roper

**Roper:** This one eyed monstrosity will give you your last hug with its long and deadly tendrils. A sedentary creature, it uses its ability to camouflage as a way to capture its prey. Watch out for stalactites in deep and dangerous caverns as they may just be ropers waiting in disguise!

# Werewolf

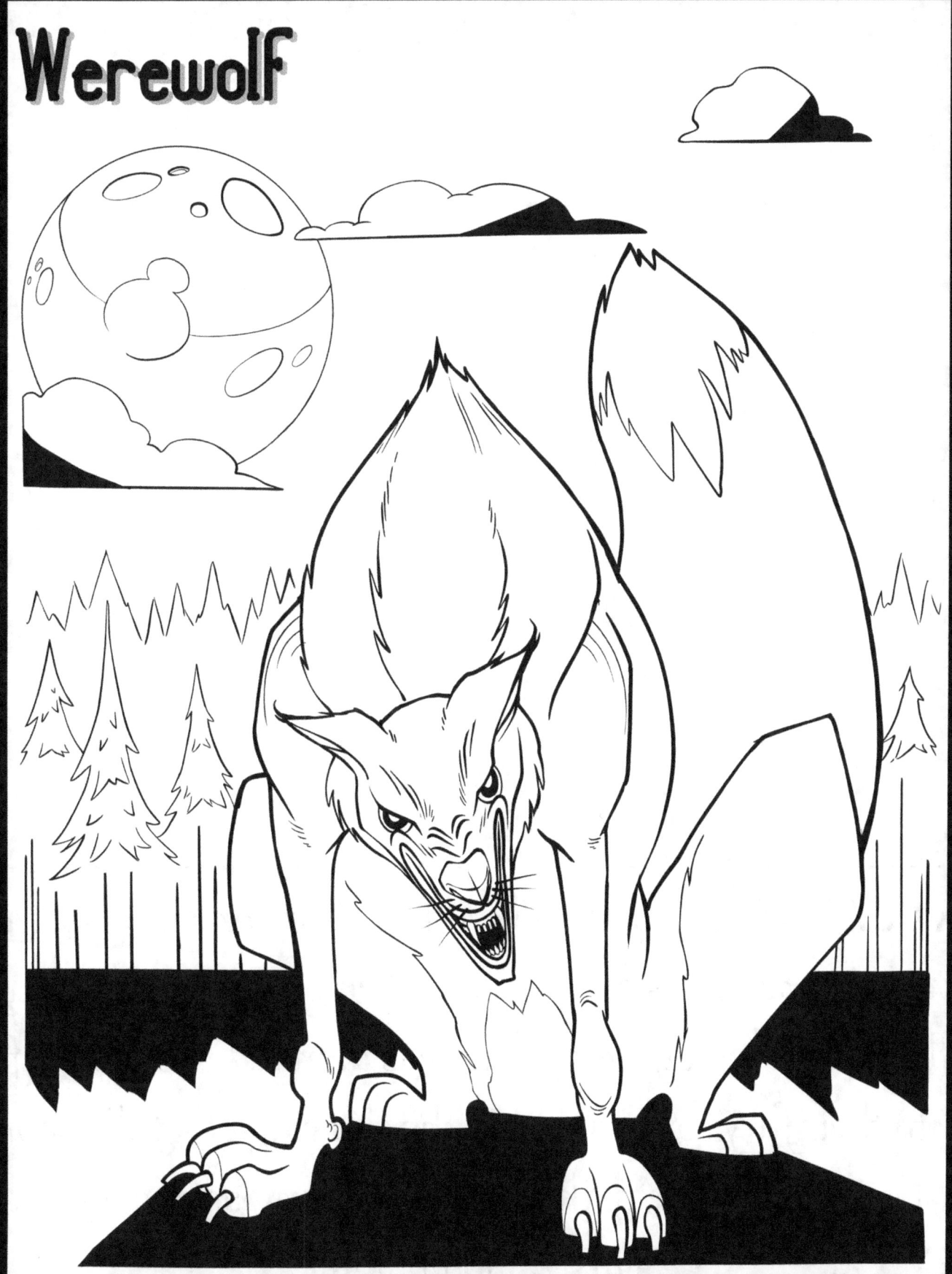

Werewolf: Aroo! When the full-moon appears, the lycanthrope comes out to play. A person who has been afflicted by the wolf-person curse is damned to shapeshift into their fury counterpart at the showing of a full-moon. Their destructive path only lasts as long as one nights cursed moon night.

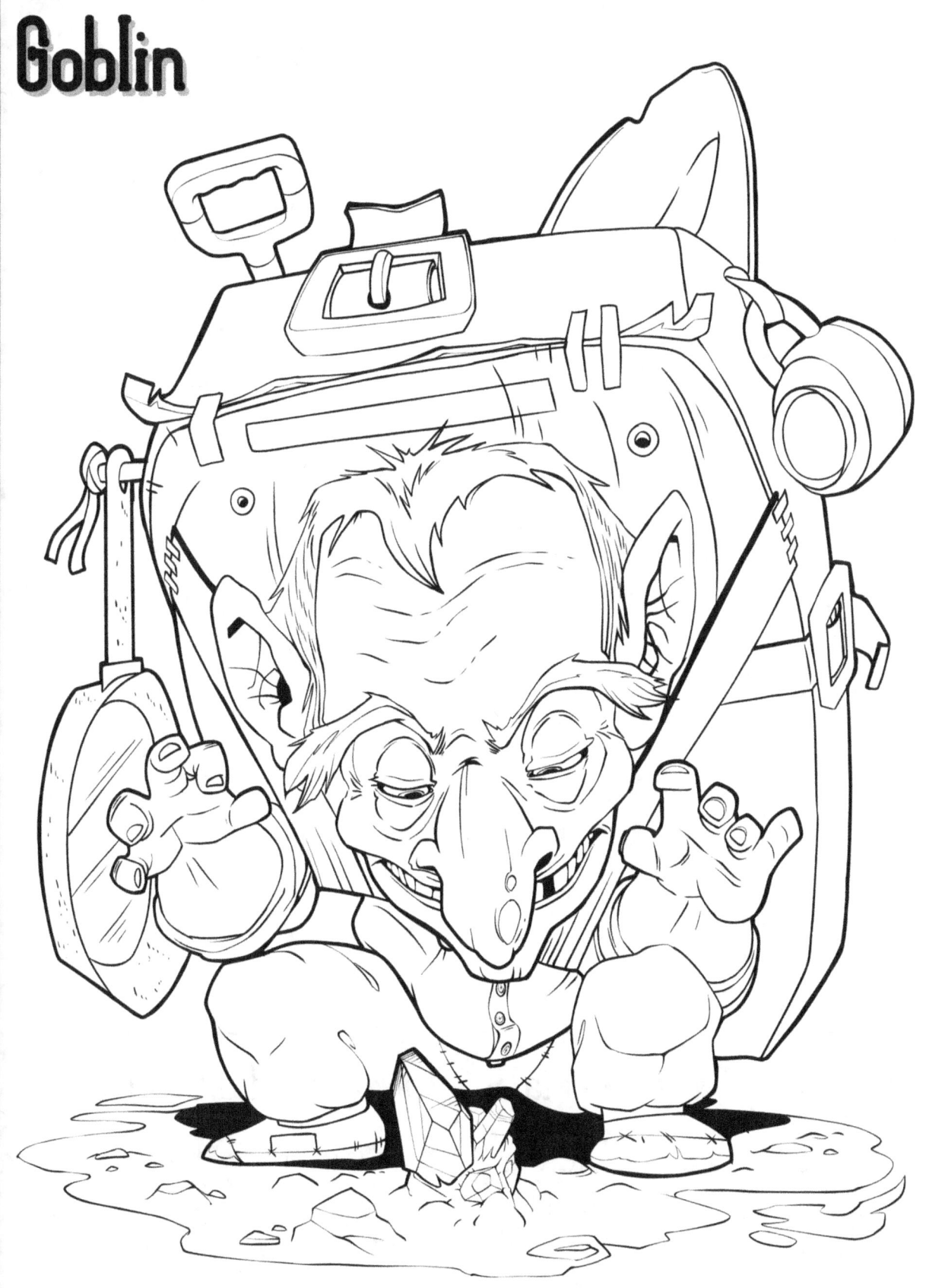

Goblin

**Goblin:** These miniature humanoid creatures are heartless to the core. The only love they may find is in the torment of others and doing whatever it takes to fulfill their insatiable greed.

# Yeti

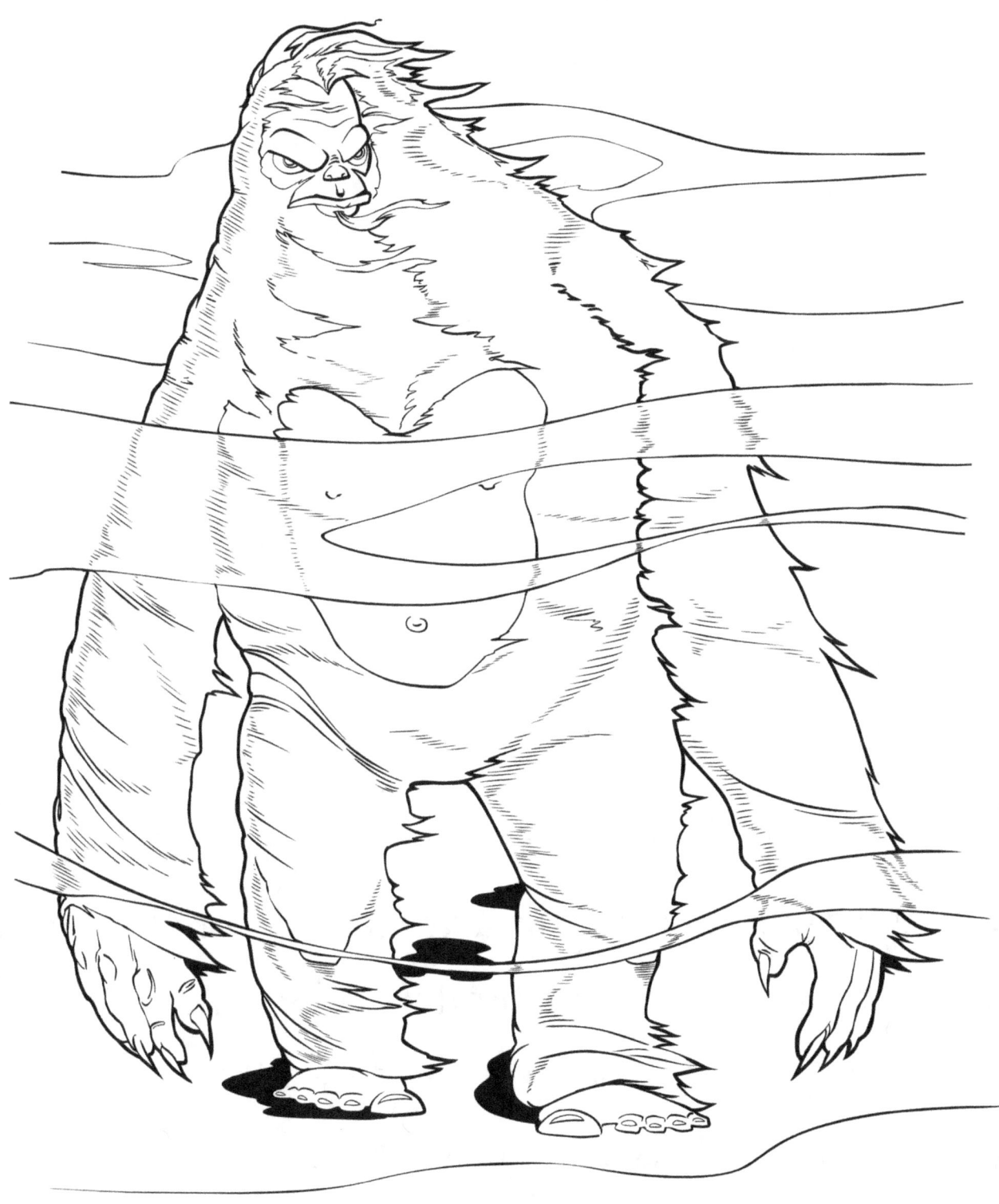

**Yeti:** Giant white haired monsters lurk in the snowy alpines searching for their next meal. If a snow mound appears to move on your mountain hike, take care, you're most likely about to be ambushed by a Yeti wanting to drag you back to is cold, dark, wintery cavern it calls home.

# Beholder

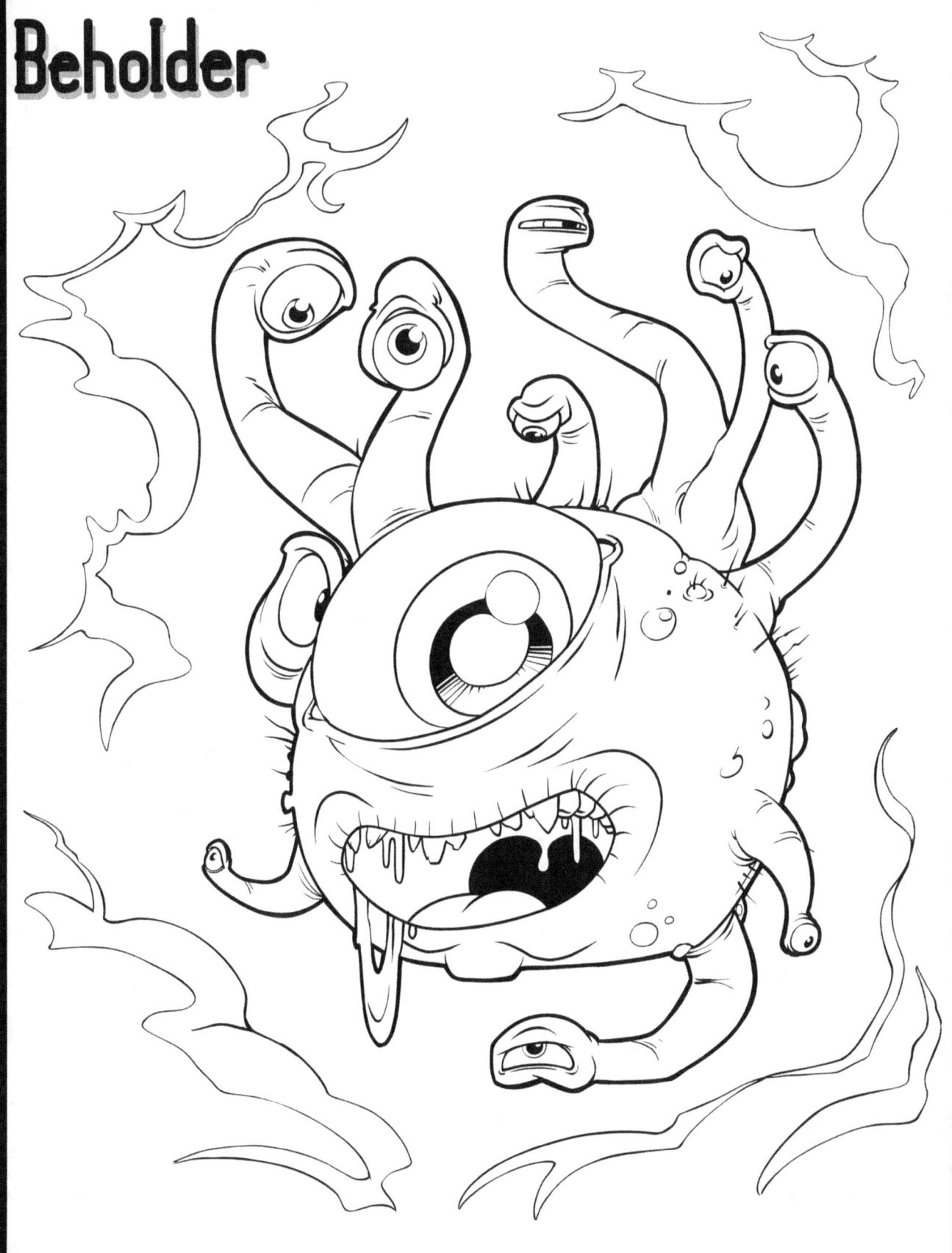

**Beholder:** Known as the sphere of many eyes, this powerful magical creature has the potential to destroy anyone that crosses its path. Do not think yourself too clever in their presence, their eyes are continuously watching and can predict your next move.